Essential Question
How do shared experiences help people adapt to change?

THE PICTURE PALACE

BY RACHEL HAYWARD
ILLUSTRATED BY DAVID OURO

CHAPTER I
THE CALL OF THE MOVIES

Frank and Joey were arguing about movie heroes. It was a well-worn theme, but one of which they never tired.

"Tarzan could not beat King Kong," scoffed Joey. "King Kong is much stronger."

"But Tarzan is a human, so his brain is bigger," said Frank. "He'd find a way to tame King Kong."

They came around the corner and stopped to gaze at the huge billboard across the street for *Call of the Wild*, starring Clark Gable.

"We have to see that movie," said Joey. But obviously, to see the movie, they needed tickets. "And for tickets, we need moolah," said Frank gloomily. These days money was hard to come by.

Frank could remember back before the stock market crash in 1929, six years earlier. He was seven then, and things were very different. He and his parents lived in a big house with a yard out back. Dad ran a factory and often came home at night with candy in his pocket or flowers for Ma.

3

Then the crash came, and the factory went out of business. Dad lost his job, and they had to sell the house. Dad ended up working three days a week in a department store. It was low pay, but Frank knew they were much luckier than some. Joey didn't talk about it much, but Frank knew that at least twice this year, Joey had come home to find his family's belongings piled out on the street and the locks changed because the rent wasn't paid.

"We need a money-making plan," said Joey.

Frank spotted a woman up ahead selling fruit on the sidewalk. "We could sell things, the way the Apple Annies do," he suggested.

"What would we sell, genius?" asked Joey scornfully. He pointed out a man washing a shop window. "What about washing windows? Do you think your mother would lend us some buckets?"

Frank grinned. "Mrs. Fisher next door might. I heard her telling Ma that you're as cute as a bug's ear." Frank sprinted off down the street with Joey hard on his heels, eager to box Frank's ears.

STOP AND CHECK

Why are Joey and Frank trying to earn money?

CHAPTER 2
SHIRLEY TEMPLE

Frank's little sister, Marie, was waiting in the hall when he arrived back home with Joey.

"Want to play jacks, Frankie?" she asked her brother hopefully.

Frank's heart sank. He loved playing with Marie, but the last thing he wanted was for Joey to think he was a weakling.

"I'm busy," he said impatiently. "Joey and I are looking for jobs." Marie's lip wobbled. To Frank's surprise, Joey dropped onto the hall rug and scooped up the jacks.

"I'll give you a game," he said, "but you have to go easy on me. I'm a beginner." He winked at Marie and scattered the jacks expertly.

Frank hovered for a minute, but Joey and Marie were absorbed in their game. Frank slouched into the kitchen.

A few moments later, the door opened, and Marie skipped in with Joey behind her. "Joey and Frankie are getting jobs!" she announced.

Ma raised an eyebrow at Frank.

"Just part-time," he explained hastily. Ma disapproved of kids quitting school early to earn money. "We need money for the movies. *Call of the Wild* is playing."

"With Clark Gable," added Joey.

Ma's expression changed completely. "Clark Gable?" she said dreamily. "Well, I guess that's okay then."

"Is Shirley Temple in it?" Marie asked. Shirley Temple, the little tap-dancing, curly-haired movie star, was Marie's heroine. Marie insisted on her fine straight hair being wound up in rags every Saturday night in a futile effort to get "curly like Shirley."

"Have a jelly sandwich, Joey," said Ma. She ran a worried eye over Joey, from his hand-me-down shirt with its fraying collar to his shoes with cardboard covering the holes in the soles. "In fact, take two," she said.

That evening when Dad came in to say good night, Frank said, "I was thinking about how many folks have lost their jobs and their homes. Is it wrong to want money just for the movies when all that bad stuff is happening?"

Dad shook his head in sympathy. "Don't worry, son," he smiled. "Movies remind us that dreams are still possible, no matter how bleak things seem." He added, "As long as we have enough to live, you can assume that I approve of your earning money to go to the movies."

STOP AND CHECK

Why is Frank worried about spending money to go to a movie?

CHAPTER 3
WASHING WINDOWS

Getting work was hard. Frank and Joey knocked on doors for an hour without any success. No one wanted to pay to have their windows washed.

"Everyone is as broke as we are," said Frank.

"You're right—we're asking the wrong people!" said Joey. "We should be across town, where the big houses are."

It was a tiring walk across town, but Frank didn't complain. He was determined to prove he was a guy Joey could rely on.

They stopped outside a big brownstone, and Joey rang the bell. A woman answered.

"Morning, ma'am!" said Joey brightly. "We were admiring all your windows, and we said, 'Maybe with our services, they could look even better.'"

Frank nodded vigorously, trying to look supportive of his friend.

"Actually, a fellow cleaned the windows just last week," the woman replied. The boys' faces fell. "Why don't you try across the street?" she suggested. "I don't think he's been there yet."

The boys were knocking on a door across the street when a gruff voice shouted, "Hey!" A large man carrying a bucket hurried toward them. "This is my block! Beat it!"

Frank was scared, but Joey yelled back, "Don't blow your wig! You don't own the street!"

The big man advanced. "I've got mouths to feed. Take a hike!" They hesitated and then took off in a flash.

When they got back to their own part of town, they stood staring at the movie billboard again.

"We'll never see that movie," Joey said gloomily.

They were interrupted by a cry. A man with a briefcase had collided with a boy on a bike. The briefcase went flying, scattering papers across the street. Quick as a flash, Joey sprinted after them, snatching them up as they whirled in the wind.

"You're fast on your feet!" the man said gratefully as Joey returned the papers. "I bet you'd be hard to beat at Bank Night."

"What's Bank Night?" Frank asked.

"It's a competition at the Palace Theater," the man explained. "You put down your name, and if they pull it out of the box, you have 60 seconds to get up on stage and claim a five-dollar prize. There's no guarantee that your name will get chosen, but if it were, I bet you'd win easily."

"A five spot!" Joey breathed. "What do you say to that, Frank?"

Frank shrugged. "What have we got to lose?"

"You shred it, wheat!" agreed Joey. "Bank Night, here we come!"

STOP AND CHECK

What does the man with the briefcase tell Joey that cheers him up?

CHAPTER 4
BANK NIGHT

The boys arrived at the Palace Theater early on Bank Night, but there was already a long line snaking up the wide front steps and into the large foyer with its ornately painted ceiling. Frank had been to the Palace before, but the gold statues and elaborate decorations still took his breath away.

At the ticket booth, a young man barely glanced at them as he rapidly wrote their names on slips of paper and inserted the slips through a slot into a locked box. The boys joined the throng of people crowding into the theater.

Inside they surveyed the crowd and frowned. They had thought the hardest part would be getting their names pulled out, but the theater was already full, with people jostling in the aisles. Getting to the front in 60 seconds would be hard.

The boys squeezed in and waited nervously.

The lights dimmed, and the organist played a fanfare. A spotlight lit the stage. The theater manager stepped out carrying the box from the ticket office. He put it down beside a large clock.

"Welcome to Bank Night!" he shouted. The crowd cheered. "You know the drill! If I call your name, you have 60 seconds to claim your prize! I'll try three names—and if no one wins, no prize!"

He unlocked the box with a flourish and pulled out a slip of paper. The organ music swelled, and the crowd fell silent.

"Bob McNeill!" shouted the manager. He hit a button, and the big clock started ticking.

A bearded man leaped up and began to struggle toward the aisle. People tried to scramble out of his way, but the clock reached 60 seconds before he got halfway to the front.

The crowd sighed with disappointment. The organ thundered again, and the manager drew another name from the box.

"Joey Mitchell!"

Joey looked stunned. Frank shook him and shoved him into the aisle. "RUN!" he yelled. But Joey could not get through the press of people.

"Go low!" Frank shouted.

Joey dropped and began to worm his way through the sea of legs. The clock ticked relentlessly—45, 46, 47 seconds. There was a commotion at the front of the theater—52, 53 seconds. Then Joey scrambled to the edge of the stage and hurled himself at the manager's feet.

The crowd went wild. Frank whooped and whistled. But the manager frowned and shook his head. "No kids!" he shouted. "Adults only!"

Frank felt sick. They had come so close! Then a voice from the front called, "But his name was in the box!"

"Give the kid the prize!" another yelled. The crowd began to boo.

"I don't make the rules," the manager said, but the crowd was chanting now. "The kid gets the prize! The kid gets the prize!"

The manager glared for a moment, then reluctantly pulled a crisp five-dollar note from his wallet. He gave it to Joey, and everyone cheered.

Outside the theater, Joey shook his head, looking dazed.

"I still can't believe it!" he said. "It's enough for the movies and still plenty left over to help out at home!" He looked seriously at Frank. "Thanks, Frank. I nominate you for best pal ever."

"Hey, Speedy," a voice called. They turned to see the man with the briefcase. "I said you were fast!" He clapped Joey on the back. "I have a proposal for you. I'm in the newspaper business, and a boy as quick as you would make a great paper boy. What do you say? An hour a day, six mornings a week, and it pays a dollar a week."

Joey nodded, lost for words. The man wrote down an address. "See you Monday, Speedy," he said. "Six o'clock. Don't be late!"

"Five dollars and a new job," Joey said as he and Frank walked home. "This might be the best day of my life!"

STOP AND CHECK

How does the man with the briefcase help Joey again?

Summarize

Use the most important details from *The Picture Palace* to summarize the story. Your graphic organizer may help you.

Text Evidence

1. What features of the text help you identify this story as historical fiction? GENRE

2. Compare and contrast the characters of Frank and Joey. COMPARE AND CONTRAST

3. What is the meaning of *quick as a flash* on page 10? Use context clues to figure out the meaning. IDIOMS

4. Write about how the Great Depression has affected Frank and Joey. How does each character respond to opportunities to make money? WRITE ABOUT READING

Compare Texts

Read about how going to the movies helped people during the 1930s.

THE GOLDEN AGE OF HOLLYWOOD

The Great Depression was a worldwide financial crisis. It lasted from 1929 to 1939. It was a time of great anxiety and poverty, and many people felt ashamed and powerless.

During this bleak time, the movies provided a place for people to gather with others and escape the harshness and dreariness of their daily lives.

Before the Depression, movies were often black and white. Sound was provided by a live musician in the theater. By the late 1920s, movie studios were able to make color "talkies" with music, sound effects, and spoken dialogue. These advances kept movies popular even during the Depression.

Some movies during the Depression reflected the harshness of the times, such as gangster movies that showed violence and poverty.

Many others, however, were musicals and romances. They showed a different world. The screwball comedy also became a popular genre. These were movies with unexpected plots, witty dialogue, and unlikely romances.

The Great Depression

The Great Depression is generally said to have started in the United States on October 29, 1929, when the stock market collapsed. Many people lost large amounts of money when the price of stocks crashed. Some businesses closed, and thousands of people lost their jobs. Unemployment reached an all-time high in 1933, when 25 percent of the country's workforce was unemployed.

During the Great Depression, soup kitchens became common, serving meals to people who could not afford to buy food.

Some of the movie theaters built in the 1920s and 1930s were so grand that they became known as "picture palaces." They had plush fabric seats, velvet stage curtains, and gold decorations.

To encourage people to come to the movies, some theaters ran special offers. Some held Bank Nights, where cash prizes were available.

Before the main movie, there were usually a short newsreel and a cartoon, and sometimes

even live music performances. A night at the movies was a complete escape from daily life.

Radio City Music Hall, built in 1932, was the largest theater in the United States at the time it opened.

Make Connections

How did watching movies together help people adapt to the big changes in their lives in the 1930s? ESSENTIAL QUESTION

Using information from *The Golden Age of Hollywood,* what do you think Joey and Frank would see and do when they went to the movies? TEXT TO TEXT

Focus on Genre

Historical Fiction Historical fiction tells us about people or events from the past. It can include real or made-up characters and events. Historical fiction has a setting, characters, and a plot.

Read and Find On page 2 of *The Picture Palace*, the author tells us when the story is set. The illustrations show where the story is set, how people dressed, and other details of daily life. The plot involves looking for part-time work to pay for a movie ticket.

Your Turn

Working with a partner, compare daily life in the 1930s with your life now. Using details from the story, list what is the same and what is different. Now imagine that your family goes back in time to live in the 1930s. Use your list to help you draw a cartoon that shows your family in the 1930s. For example, you might draw a typical day without the modern conveniences of TVs, dishwashers, and computers. Write a caption for your cartoon to explain what the cartoon shows.